Jewish
IN AMERICA

Barbara Sheen

ReferencePoint
Press®

San Diego, CA

© 2021 ReferencePoint Press, Inc.
Printed in the United States

For more information, contact:
ReferencePoint Press, Inc.
PO Box 27779
San Diego, CA 92198
www.ReferencePointPress.com

LIBRARY OF CONGRESS CATALOGING-IN-PUBLICATION DATA

Names: Sheen, Barbara, author.
Title: Jewish in America / by Barbara Sheen.
Description: San Diego, CA : ReferencePoint Press, 2021. | Series: Bias in America | Includes bibliographical references and index.
Identifiers: LCCN 2019054377 (print) | LCCN 2019054378 (ebook) | ISBN 9781682828953 (library binding) | ISBN 9781682828960 (ebook)
Subjects: LCSH: Antisemitism--United States--History. | United States--Ethnic relations.
Classification: LCC DS146.U6 S47 2021 (print) | LCC DS146.U6 (ebook) | DDC 305.892/4073--dc23
LC record available at https://lccn.loc.gov/2019054377
LC ebook record available at https://lccn.loc.gov/2019054378

CONTENTS

A Growing Problem

On August 12, 2017, as Jews worshipped in Congregation Beth El, a synagogue in Charlottesville, Virginia, a band of far-right extremists wielding semiautomatic weapons marched outside the synagogue. Many of the marchers chanted *"Sieg Heil,"* a Nazi victory cry, and waved flags imprinted with swastikas and other Nazi symbols.

Sequestered within the synagogue's windowless sanctuary, the worshippers were unaware of what was going on outside. But when the services ended and the congregants left the confines of the sanctuary, a wave of fear flowed over them. "We're standing there at 11:30, and someone points [outside], and there's a group of racists coming down the street," said congregant Geoff Schmelkin. "I came to the window, and sure enough, you could see the skinhead types walking past the synagogue. It strikes a chord for Jewish people to see those things on the streets outside the synagogue. For a lot of Jews, it's our worst nightmare come true."[1]

In an effort to avoid a confrontation with the demonstrators, the congregants slipped out through the back exit, taking the synagogue's sacred Torah scrolls with them. As they left, they became aware of other extremists driving by the synagogue, spitting at the building and shouting anti-Semitic slurs.

The demonstrators were part of the Unite the Right rally, a protest rally organized by a number of far-right, or alt-right, white nationalist extremist groups. The rally, which ended in violence and the death of a female counterprotester, was attended by about five hundred extremists who shared a common hatred for Jews and other minorities. Besides parading around the synagogue, they also marched through Charlottesville giving the stiff-arm Nazi salute; waving Nazi flags; carrying posters that claimed "Jews are Satan's children"; and chanting, "The Jews will not replace us," "Heil Hitler," and other Nazi slogans. They also shouted other racist slurs aimed at insulting other minorities. Many were armed with guns, shields, and clubs.

What Is Anti-Semitism?

The Unite the Right rally was not an isolated occurrence. Hateful actions and rhetoric against Jews in the United States are increasing. These incidents are not motivated by individual conflicts but rather by a form of prejudice known as anti-Semitism. The Anti-Defamation League (ADL), a Jewish anti-hate organization, defines *anti-Semitism* as "the belief or behavior hostile toward Jews just because they are Jewish."[2]

Anti-Semitism is not a new prejudice. It has been in existence for thousands of years. It is based on various irrational conspiracy theories that blame Jews, as a group, for all of society's problems. No matter how illogical these theories are, they have been the rationale for discrimination, oppression, and violence against Jews throughout history. According to David Samuels, a Jewish writer, "Anti-Semitism is a degenerative thought-virus that makes people crazy by promising to explain everything that happens in the world with reference to a single prime mover—the Jews. Because anti-Semitism is a conspiracy theory . . . it is fatal to rational thinking."[3]

> "Anti-Semitism is a degenerative thought-virus that makes people crazy by promising to explain everything that happens in the world with reference to a single prime mover—the Jews."[3]
>
> —David Samuels, a Jewish writer

One person died after a man drove his car into counterprotesters during the Unite the Right rally in Charlottesville, Virginia, on August 12, 2017. Participants in the rally displayed Nazi symbols and carried signs featuring anti-Semitic slogans.

Reports of anti-Semitic incidents compiled by the Federal Bureau of Investigation (FBI) and by the ADL provide statistics on the escalating climate of anti-Semitism in the United States. The ADL recorded 1,986 attacks against Jews and Jewish institutions in 2017 and 1,879 attacks in 2018. Although the total number of incidents decreased in 2018, that year's total is still 48 percent greater than the number of incidents in 2016 and 99 percent greater than in 2015. Incidents that are tracked include assaults, harassment (which includes bullying), and vandalism. Indeed, hostility toward Jews is becoming increasingly common. According to the FBI, although Jews make up only 2.2 percent of the American population, 58.2 percent of all hate crimes motivated by religious bias target Jews. This makes Jews the most widely attacked religious group in the nation.

The Spillover Effect of Hatred

Although anti-Semitic hostility most directly affects Jews, bias and hostility of this sort tends to not be limited to only one group.

Anti-Semitism thrives in societies that feel threatened by and are intolerant of anyone who is different. And, as bigotry toward any group grows, intolerance toward other groups, whether based on religion, race, or sexual preferences, usually becomes more acceptable too. As Deborah E. Lipstadt, an author and a professor of Jewish history at Emory University, writes,

> Some . . . may be inclined to think that only Jews should be concerned. That would be a mistake. . . . The existence of prejudice in any of its forms is a threat to all those who value an inclusive, democratic, and multicultural society. . . . If Jews are being targeted with hateful rhetoric and prejudice, other minorities should not feel immune; this is not likely to end with Jews. And, conversely, if other minority groups are being targeted with hatred and prejudice, Jews should not feel immune; this is not likely to end with these groups either. Antisemitism flourishes in a society that is intolerant of others, be they immigrants or racial or religious minorities. . . . Like a fire set by an arsonist, passionate hatred and conspiratorial worldviews reach well beyond their intended target. They are not rationally contained. But even if the anti-Semites were to confine their venom to Jews, the existence of Jew-hatred within a society is an indication that something about the entire society is amiss. No healthy society harbors extensive antisemitism—or any other form of hatred.[4]

CHAPTER ONE

Promises Made, Promises Broken

Jews have lived in America since the seventeenth century. From colonial times, they have enjoyed freedom and opportunities that have allowed them to prosper. But life for Jews in America has not been without challenges. Their religion and culture have marked them as different from the Christian majority. Some Americans distrust those who are different and discriminate against them. Consequently, bias against Jews has always existed in America. During some periods it has been out in the open; during others, it has been more subtle. In recent years, overt bias toward Jews has resurfaced.

Changing Times, Changing Levels of Bias

Some of the earliest Jewish immigrants settled in the Dutch colony of New Amsterdam (now New York City) after fleeing religious persecution in Europe. Peter Stuyvesant, the director-general of New Amsterdam, was known to be hostile toward Jews. He wanted to prohibit Jews from residing in New Amsterdam, insisting that they were notorious for their greed and dishonesty. Officials in the Netherlands overruled him. The newcomers were permitted to take up residence as long as they conducted their religious activities in private. Jews soon came to live in the other colonies, where they often faced restrictions on their personal rights and religious practices. Still, by the end of the American Revolution, Jews were firmly established in America.

The creation of the US Constitution, which spelled out the rules that governed the new nation, brought about improvements in the lives of Jews in America. Rather than establishing a national religion and expecting all Americans to practice it, as most nations did at the time, the Constitution gave all Americans the freedom to worship as they chose without fear of persecution. It also prohibited the government from favoring one religion over another. Plus, it granted Jews full citizenship, which allowed Jewish men to vote, serve in the military, hold public office, and own property. This is significant because the Constitution did not grant citizenship to African slaves or Native Americans. Jews, however, were considered to be white Europeans, and as such, they were granted these rights. Indeed, the Constitution offered Jews freedom and security that were unheard-of in the rest of the world. In a 1790 letter to the Hebrew Congregation of Newport, Rhode Island, George Washington pledged:

> The government of the United States which gives to bigotry no sanction, to persecution no assistance, requires only that they who live under its protection demean [conduct] themselves as good citizens. . . . May the children of the Stock of Abraham [the Jews], who dwell in this land, continue to merit and enjoy the good will of the other inhabitants, while everyone shall sit in safety under his own vine and fig tree, and there shall be none to make him afraid.[5]

From then on, until the late nineteenth century, even though Jews were often looked down on, they did not face blatant anti-Semitism. Nevertheless, it was not uncommon for Jews to be insulted, marginalized, denied credit by banks, and subjected to religious zealots who tried to convert them. However, these

In the early twentieth century, an estimated 3 million Jewish immigrants fleeing poverty and religious persecution in eastern Europe flooded into the United States. Their first stop in their new country was the immigration processing center at Ellis Island, New York (pictured).

things paled in comparison to the violent persecution Jews faced in Europe. In America, Jews were largely allowed to live, work, and worship in peace. Many became merchants and prospered financially. Most adopted the American way of life and—at least outwardly—seemed like other Americans.

Open Hatred

Conditions changed for Jews at the start of the twentieth century, when an estimated 3 million Jewish immigrants fleeing poverty and religious persecution in eastern Europe flooded into the United States. Unlike their assimilated peers, these Jews were uneducated, poor, and extremely devout. They dressed differently and adhered to customs that seemed strange by American standards. Many Americans mistrusted them. Their strangeness, combined with the rise of nationalism and fascism in Europe, influenced American attitudes and gave rise to intense bias toward other Jews living in the United States. This hostility continued throughout the first half of the twentieth century. Jews were now thought of as being part of a separate and inferior racial group and were generally not accepted by society. In fact, they were so unwelcome that the federal government passed a law restricting Jewish immigration in 1924.

Public institutions and private organizations began limiting (or, in some cases, prohibiting) Jewish participation. Some educational institutions set quotas limiting the enrollment of Jewish students. For example, Jewish enrollment in many top colleges and universities was limited to 1 percent of the student body in 1945. Jews were also socially segregated. They were barred from many clubs, hotels, restaurants, beaches, and recreational facilities. Meyer Lesser, a Jew who traveled through the United States during the 1930s, recalls, "I saw plenty of signs 'No Jews, no dogs permitted.'"[6]

> **"I saw plenty of signs 'No Jews, no dogs permitted.'"[6]**
>
> —Meyer Lesser, a Jew who traveled around the United States during the 1930s

Jews also felt the sting of discrimination in their work and home life. Many communities adopted zoning regulations that prohibited Jews from living in certain neighborhoods. Likewise, employment opportunities for Jews were strictly limited, with many businesses, law firms, educational institutions, and medical facilities refusing to hire them. As Ethel Wool Kagen, a Jewish woman, remembers, "I applied at the telephone company [in 1921], and if I had put on the application that I was Jewish I could never have gotten the job. They didn't employ Jews."[7] In addition, Jews were not admitted to many hospitals. Consequently, it was not uncommon for Jews in larger cities to establish hospitals to serve the Jewish community.

Faced with discrimination, many Jews did whatever they could to be more readily accepted by society. Although most did not deny their religion, they did not advertise it either. Some anglicized their surnames so that they could not be easily identified as Jews. This resulted in anti-Semites charging

> **"I applied at the telephone company [in 1921], and if I had put on the application that I was Jewish I could never have gotten the job. They didn't employ Jews."[7]**
>
> —Ethel Wool Kagen, a Jewish woman

Who Are American Jews?

There are currently about 7.2 million Jews living in the United States, composing about 2 percent of the nation's total population. This makes the United States home to more Jews than any other country in the world, including Israel, which is home to approximately 6.7 million Jews. Of America's Jews, an estimated 1.6 million are children.

Jews live in every state. The majority (65 percent) reside in New York, California, Florida, New Jersey, and Illinois. With an estimated 1.5 million Jews, or about 23 percent of the national Jewish population, New York has the largest Jewish population, and South Dakota, with only about 250 Jews, has the smallest. Most Jews live in large metropolitan areas. Cities with large Jewish populations include New York City, Los Angeles, San Francisco, Boston, Philadelphia, and Baltimore.

Racially, not all Jews are Caucasian. In a 2019 study, social scientists at Brandeis University's Steinhardt Social Research Institute found that 89 percent of American Jews identify racially as white. Eleven percent identify as people of color. Of the latter group, 2 percent identify as black, 5 percent as Hispanic, and 4 percent as another ethnicity.

No matter their ethnicity, Jews are usually well educated and tend to be politically progressive. Approximately, 61 percent have a bachelor's degree or higher. Politically, 42 percent of Jewish Americans identify as liberals, 38 percent as moderates, and 20 percent as conservatives.

that Jews were schemers. Indeed, propaganda maligning Jews was widespread. Influential followers of Nazism, such as automobile executive Henry Ford and Father Charles Coughlin, a Catholic priest who hosted a radio show that reached millions of listeners, used the media to turn popular opinion against Jews. Newspapers and magazines commonly printed anti-Semitic articles and cartoons accusing Jews of undermining moral values, secretly controlling global politics and financial systems, and being responsible for the death of Jesus Christ. In fact, the latter accusation was part of many church teachings. Sylvia Skoler Portnoy, a Jew who grew up during the 1940s, recalls how her gentile (non-Jewish) peers treated her: "I remember their coming home from catechism after being taught the Jews killed Jesus and calling me a Christ-killer. I remember sitting on the front porch with my brother and the kids we normally played with sitting on a porch across the street and yelling at us, 'Dirty Jew, Christ-killer.'"[8]

According to historian Leonard Dinnerstein, bias against Jews became so widespread that, by 1944, 24 percent of Americans named Jews as the greatest threat America faced, far exceeding the perceived threat from the Japanese (9 percent) or Germans (6 percent), with whom the United States was at war. White supremacist groups such as the Ku Klux Klan (KKK), which had previously directed their activities against America's black population, turned some of their terror tactics toward Jews. Members of the KKK assaulted Jews and destroyed their property. Brenda

Members of the white supremacist group the Ku Klux Klan march in Washington, DC, in 1927. Originally formed to intimidate African Americans in the wake of the Civil War, in the twentieth century the group turned some of its terror tactics toward Jews.

Robinson Wolchok, a Jewish woman who grew up in Georgia, recalls, "My mother told me stories of how the Ku Klux Klan would march down the street during the Depression [in the 1930s] when she was a young girl. They lived above the store, and they would run and hide in the back."[9] Jews also faced physical assaults from prejudiced individuals and roving gangs of youths.

Subtle Discrimination

After the Holocaust, which is the name given to the systematic murder of about 6 million Jews during World War II by the Nazis, many Americans became more sympathetic toward the plight of the Jews. As author and political scientist Richard L. Rubin explains,

> This extraordinary change can only be fully understood as a profound moral reaction to the ultimate result of discrimination—the Holocaust. . . . Horrific details of the death camps worked their way into American consciousness . . . piercing the souls of an American public that had too easily closed its eyes to the rampant discrimination against domestic racial and religious minorities.[10]

As a result, between the 1950s and the early 2000s, outright discrimination and blatant anti-Semitic activity in the United States lessened, but it did not disappear entirely. Jews were still excluded from many recreational and social clubs. But, unlike in earlier years, they faced less overt hostility. Wolchok recollects,

> I had only one real anti-Semitic experience growing up in Savannah. That was in high school, when a Christian friend put my name up for a sorority. "I don't think that's a problem," she said when I told her I was Jewish. After speaking to her president, however, she called me back. "I'm sorry," she said. "It's not that we don't like you. It's just that our customs are so different from yours."[11]

Restricting Where Jews Could Live

In the early through mid-twentieth century, racially restrictive covenants or regulations kept property owners from selling, leasing, or renting property in certain neighborhoods to Jews and nonwhite individuals. For instance, a 1946 restrictive covenant on lakefront property in Minneapolis stipulated that the property could not be sold or leased to any people of African, Chinese, Japanese, Arabic, or Jewish descent, among other minorities. There was no time limit on restrictive covenants. These regulations applied to both the original and future sale or lease of a property; thereby, legally, keeping "undesirable" people such as Jews out of a neighborhood indefinitely. If a seller violated the covenant, he or she could be sued.

The regulations helped attract white, non-Jewish buyers and renters who did not want to live in integrated communities. They were supported by the real estate industry, land developers, and banks, as well as by the federal housing authority, who believed the rules would promote neighborhood stability.

Racially restrictive covenants were common until 1968, when the Fair Housing Act, which ended discrimination in housing, was enacted. While they were legal, restrictive covenants segregated neighborhoods and kept Jews and other minorities from fully integrating into American society.

In other ways, Jews were gaining greater acceptance. The passage of the Civil Rights Act in 1964 opened many doors. It made religious, racial, and ethnic discrimination illegal. Under protection of the new law, Jews could live wherever they wanted, attend prestigious universities, and work in every field. As a result, many received advanced degrees, became quite successful in their careers, and did well financially. By the start of the twenty-first century, most Jews were living typical American lives. Believing that they were finally fully accepted into US society, many assumed anti-Semitism was a thing of the past. Marc Angel, a rabbi who grew up in Seattle, remembers, "Although we knew about the tragedies of the Jews throughout history and had observances that reminded us of them, these were remote events. We thought we were lucky. We thought everything we had was the best. We thought Jews were the happiest, luckiest people in the world."[12]

Growing Extremism

Even during these good times, an undercurrent of anti-Semitism persists—especially among white nationalist groups and those who affiliate with them. Most of these individuals embrace irrational neo-Nazi conspiracy theories that demonize Jews and blame them for all kinds of issues. "Anti-Semitism is part and parcel of the movement," explains Eric Ward, a civil rights strategist who infiltrated one of these groups. "It is the oxygen and the fuel that allows the engine of the alt-right and nationalist movement to thrive and breathe. It is the paper upon which all the other forms of bigotry are being written upon."[13]

Most such extremists believe that white Christians are superior to other ethnic, religious, or racial groups and therefore should have dominance over them. However, the growing acceptance and political clout of blacks, Hispanics, the LGBTQ community, and other historically oppressed groups in the United States has changed the balance of power. As a result, extremists feel that their position in society is under assault. They baselessly blame Jews, who they believe secretly control the government, for elevating persecuted groups to the detriment of white Christians. Author and journalist Jonathan Weisman explains:

They look around and see groups not their own rising in stature or power or just numbers: Italians or Irish in past eras, blacks or Hispanics now, people the bigots feel superior to but somehow beaten by. How could these people who are so beneath us be beating us? the bigots ask, and begin to look for some unseen power orchestrating their decline. . . . Invariably, they latch on to the Jews.[14]

Therefore, many extremists believe that it is their duty to defend themselves against Jews. As Jeff Schoep, the leader of a neo-Nazi group, insists, "It is the Jew that is the true enemy of all humanity on this planet! All the other races and racial problems we have go back to the Jew, and the focus should never be removed from them."[15] Defense against the perceived Jewish enemy includes violence. For example, in 2018 the ADL attributed 249 violent anti-Semitic incidents to extremist groups or individuals. This was 13 percent of the total number of anti-Semitic incidents in that year and the highest level of such incidents connected to extremists in fourteen years.

New Boldness

Moreover, these groups have become much bolder in their rhetoric and actions. Before the 2016 candidacy and election of Donald Trump, these groups existed outside the mainstream. But Trump, whose policies and blunt language resonate with many of these

The leaders of many white supremacist groups endorsed Donald Trump (pictured) for president in the 2016 election. Trump has claimed that he is not anti-Semitic, but he accepted such endorsements and has not distanced himself from such groups.

extremists, appears to have emboldened them and made their ideology more acceptable to society at large. "I think Trump was a big legitimizer," says William Regnery, a founder of the National Policy Institute, a white nationalist think tank. "White nationalism went from being a conversation you could hold in a bathroom to a front parlor."[16]

Many leaders of these groups endorsed Trump's candidacy. For instance, in an April 2016 speech, white nationalist leader Andrew Anglin told his followers, "The day is coming when we're going to tear down the hoax [Holocaust] memorial in Berlin and replace it with a statue of Hitler 1,000 feet tall. . . . Jews, Blacks and lesbians will be leaving America if Trump gets elected—and he's happy about it. This alone is enough reason to put your entire heart and soul into supporting this man."[17]

Whether or not Trump shares such views is questionable. He has adamantly denied being anti-Semitic. In fact, he told a reporter during a 2017 news conference, "I am the least anti-Semitic person that you've ever seen in your entire life."[18] Although this may be true, as a presidential candidate Trump accepted the endorsement of neo-Nazi and white nationalist leaders. And he did not distance himself from them after he was elected. Therefore, feeling accepted by those in power, these extremists have become more blatant in attacking Jews.

Indeed, the current hostility toward Jews makes it obvious that anti-Semitism in the United States has not disappeared. Throughout US history, Jews have been the object of bias. This bias persists today, threatening Jews and society at large. "Anti-Semitism," says Weisman, "is a pestilence that has survived millennia, raging at some times, retreating at other times into carriers that have passed it on in silence through generations. The questions, then, are what triggered its latest outbreak, how were we again caught unawares, and what are we going to do about it?"[19]

CHAPTER TWO

Insults, Bullying, and Discrimination on Campus

Jews of all ages experience anti-Semitism. Jewish children, teens, and young adults, in particular, have been the target of insults, bullying, and discrimination in schools and on college campuses. Not only is this mistreatment hurtful, but it also singles out young Jews as being different from the majority, attacks their dignity, and marginalizes them. Although this type of hostile activity has surged in recent years, these abuses usually do not physically endanger the victims. For this reason, in many cases, they are ignored or discounted by those in authority. Indeed, harassing Jewish students has become increasingly acceptable in some segments of US society. A Jewish teen describes her experience:

> My entire life, my mother has told me to grow thicker skin—that I need to block out the nasty words and comments. If you react, she says, it only gives them more power. I recognize there is truth to her words—wisdom, even—but exactly how thick must my skin get? At times, it feels like no matter how tall I stand—how steadfast and strong and tree-like—my peers, and even adults, blow harder and harder with their antisemitic comments each time."[20]

The teen lives in a small city in North Carolina where almost everyone is Christian. Many of the townspeople have had little contact with Jews, view them as different, and accept anti-Semitic stereotypes and conspiracy theories as fact. As a result, the teen regularly experiences anti-Semitism in her high school where she is one of only a few Jewish students. As she explains:

> Some comments from my peers stem purely from ignorance, like the time a friend told me I'd ace our economics and tax law units simply because I'm Jewish. (Newsflash: I'm not good with money because I'm Jewish, Kathy. It's because I find calculus a breeze.) There was also the time when a classmate told me I was a "lizard person" who controls the banks, the news and the government. This one was so outlandish that I couldn't help but laugh. . . . The more blatantly antisemitic comments I've endured range from my fellow marching band members telling me Adolf Hitler should have "tried just a little bit harder" to a boy with a Confederate flag T-shirt and MAGA [Trump slogan, "Make America Great Again"] hat informing me that all of "my kind" would need to be exterminated in order to reinstate peace, return Israel to the Christian people and, above all, revive Jesus. . . . I still can't help but feel the Jewish community is isolated because we are seen as "other." This feeling slams into me with the negative comments about my Jewish identity.[21]

Mistreatment by Other Students

Not only do Jewish students too often face insulting anti-Semitic rhetoric, they are also often mocked, harassed, bullied, and intimidated by their peers simply because of their religion. In 2017, for instance, Jewish middle and high school students in East Brunswick, New Jersey, reported receiving anti-Semitic notes that advised them to kill themselves and finding swastikas and Nazi graf-

fiti drawn on their desks and lockers. In one school, non-Jewish students proclaimed and observed "Kick a Jew Day."

These types of incidents are not isolated to East Brunswick. They are occurring all over the country. According to the ADL there were 231 instances of harassment of Jewish elementary through high school students by their peers in 2017 and 341 such instances in 2018. These incidents include verbal and written insults and other expressions of harassment as well as anti-Semitic bullying, all of which can negatively affect victims' emotional well-being. Dakota Cohen, a young Jewish man, was a target of anti-Semitic bullying. He recalls his experience:

> The bullying started my first year in third grade and continued my entire career in school. It progressively got worse over time and by middle school I was made fun of heavily for being Jewish and overweight. I had coins thrown at me [an allusion to a stereotype of Jews being stingy] and asked to go retrieve them. I was called, "dirty Jew, stupid Jew, kike.". . . This happened every day and when you are this young—this is your entire life. . . . Life was just so unbearable. I thought about suicide, but I never acted on it.[22]

Being Different

Blogger Erin Konheim Mandras is a Jewish athlete who played soccer through-out her school career. Following college, she went on to play semiprofessional women's soccer and later became a collegiate soccer coach. In a blog post, she recalls the discrimination she faced as a Jewish athlete:

> Throughout my entire career soccer was never scheduled on Christ-mas Day or Easter Day, nor should it have been. However, soccer al-ways conflicted with the holiest Jewish holidays in the year, Rosh Ha-shanah and Yom Kippur; both of which always fell right in the middle of fall season. I was raised in a household where we observed these holidays, my father didn't work, we didn't go to school, and we didn't participate in extracurricular activities. My team was scheduled to play in the best tournament, at the time, in Washington D.C. over Co-lumbus Day weekend. My coach's rule was a missed practice would result in not starting the next game. It was the most significant year to be evaluated by college coaches. The practice prior to the tournament was Yom Kippur, and I had to miss. That same day, my teammate missed practice to go on a college visit. My coach punished me for missing, and sat me out to start the first game of the tournament, but he excused her. There may be exceptions to rules. And, to me, a Jew-ish holiday was an excusable reason to miss a sporting commitment, and not suffer consequences.

Erin Konheim Mandras, "How Being Jewish and an Athlete Contributed to My Eventual Downfall (Part 2)," *Kick the Scale* (blog), March 21, 2016. http://kickthescale.com.

Jewish elementary school students have also been targeted by other kids. In 2017 an anti-Semitic death threat was circulated among fourth graders in an elementary school in Northern Cali-fornia. Moreover, mistreating and insulting Jewish youngsters is not limited to individual bullies.

In many cases, groups of students engage in collective anti-Semitic behavior. In fact, groups of students imitating Nazi behavior and joking about their support for Nazism, Hitler, and the Holocaust have become widespread. In 2019 groups of students from three different Southern California high schools posted photos and videos of themselves on social media in which they engaged in hate speech, gave the Nazi straight-arm salute, and sang a Nazi marching song. Other groups have been photographed giving the Nazi salute at a Wisconsin prom, a Minnesota school dance, a San Francisco pep rally, and during senior picture day in Houston, among other occurrences.

Misguided Educators

In some cases, teachers, coaches, school administrators, and other educators mistreat Jewish students. These abuses occur for a number of reasons and may be intentional or unintentional. In some cases, those in authority do not take anti-Semitic behavior seriously. Consequently, they may be slow to respond or may not respond appropriately. Take the 2019 case of a Jewish high school student in New Jersey who was spat on and called a "Jew dyke" by a classmate while a group of other girls looked on and cheered. After the student reported the incident to a school administrator, all the girls (including the victim) were called into the office, but the only person who was reprimanded was the victim. She was accused of being overly sensitive, and the case was closed. Another young Jewish woman reports that while she and her older brother were growing up in Arizona, they were repeatedly bullied and harassed because they were Jews. After months of being pushed around, bombarded by anti-Semitic slurs, and having swastikas drawn on his homework assignments, her brother fought back. He was suspended from school for fighting, but his tormentors were not punished for their actions. Commenting about similar incidents, Jay P. Greene, a professor of education policy at the University of Arkansas, maintains,

"We have trusted public schools far too much to protect us when the evidence suggests that these local governmental institutions are not reliable partners in combating antisemitism."[23]

In other instances, teachers have given inappropriate assignments that distress Jewish students and sometimes even encourage anti-Semitic behavior. In 2017, for instance, students in a New York high school social studies class were divided into two groups. Students in one group were asked to write an essay, from the perspective of a Nazi official, defending the extermination of the Jews during the Holocaust. Those in the second group were asked to write an essay opposing it. Although two students reported feeling very uncomfortable with the assignment, the teacher defended it, as did the state education commissioner at first. Eventually, the school district apologized for the assignment, but not before the media, lawmakers, and anti-hate organizations got involved. In its opposition to the assignment, Evan Bernstein, the regional director of the ADL's New York–New Jersey branch, said, "There is no assignment that could ever be given to students that even hints at a balanced perspective to the horrors of Nazi actions during the Holocaust. . . . When developing curricula, educators must recognize the detrimental impact of such role-playing activities and understand the deep sensitivities surrounding such a topic."[24]

In a similar occurrence in 2019, a Tennessee fifth grader was assigned the role of Adolf Hitler as part of a living history exhibit. During rehearsal, the student gave the Nazi salute and victory shout. About one dozen of his classmates responded by saluting and shouting back. Upset by their actions, a Jewish girl shouted for her classmates to put their arms down. The girl then turned to the teacher, demanding that the teacher stop this behavior. In response, the teacher removed the girl from the classroom, accused her of being disrespectful, and ordered her not to address the subject again. The girl was then sent to the office to be disciplined. The other students continued to make Nazi salutes on the playground and in the halls for the rest of the school year. Once again, it was only after the media and various organizations became involved that the school agreed to no longer include a student portraying Hitler or the Nazi salute in future presentations.

Holiday Pressures

Other actions are less overt but still hostile. These may be attributed to insensitivity or lack of awareness of Jewish culture and traditions on the part of some educators. Although almost all school districts do not hold classes on the Christian holidays of Christmas and Good Friday, most—with the exception of a few ethnically diverse school districts—hold classes on the Jewish high holidays of Rosh Hashanah and Yom Kippur. Nor do all schools make special

Jewish students in most American public school districts often must miss school to celebrate holidays because classes are held on those days. In the Jewish school pictured here, students participate in a service before the high holy day of Rosh Hashanah, also known as the Jewish New Year.

accommodations, such as giving Jewish students who observe these holidays a reasonable amount of time to make up missed assignments. In fact, it is not unusual for schools to schedule tests, picture days, mandatory team practices, and important extracurricular activities on the Jewish high holidays.

For example, Rachel Hale, a Jewish high school student, reports that her school held its Big 10 College Night on the night of Yom Kippur. This puts a lot of pressure on Jewish students not to miss school. As Hale writes,

> Having school off on Christmas is a no-brainer; but important Jewish holidays, such as Rosh Hashanah and Yom Kippur, are barely an afterthought on school boards' minds. . . . For some Jewish students, missing school for important holidays is nothing out of the ordinary. But for others, the stress of missing multiple classes, tests, and extracurricular activities outweighs the importance of services. Some teachers are not understanding of the holiday's religious significance and do not consider the day an excused absence. . . . Why should students have to choose between prayer and planning for college? Why should they have to choose between going to after-school activities and attending services? . . . School, as important as it may be, should never impose upon our right to pray and our right to a substantial Jewish faith.[25]

Trouble on College Campuses

Verbal abuse, marginalization, discrimination, and harassment follow many Jewish students onto college campuses. This mistreatment originates from multiple sources. Some abuses come from supporters of the Boycott, Divestment, and Sanctions (BDS) movement. BDS supporters are opposed to the Israeli government's treatment of Palestinians. They support boycotting Israeli businesses, products, and public events in which Israelis participate. They

Anti-Semitism on College Campuses

Many Jewish college students are routinely confronted by anti-Semitism. Below are a few of the many anti-Semitic incidents that have occurred on American college campuses in the past few years:

- Mock eviction notices were posted on dorm room doors of Jewish students at Emory University in Atlanta and at New York University in 2019.
- A student at Stanford University in Palo Alto, California, was questioned about how her Jewish identity would conflict with her serving in student government in 2015.
- Graffiti in a campus bathroom at the University of California, Berkeley, declared that Jews should be sent to the gas chamber in 2015.
- Students at Barnard College in New York received emails claiming that Jews caused the 9/11 terrorist attacks in 2018.
- A professor at the University of Michigan refused to write letters of recommendation for Jewish students wanting to study in Israel in 2018.
- Swastikas were painted on the door of a Jewish fraternity house at the University of California, Davis in 2016.
- Student groups at the California Polytechnic Institute in San Luis Obispo demanded an increase in funding for all cultural clubs—with the exception of organizations that support Israel in 2018.
- Two dozen anti-Semitic posters were found on the campus of Tufts University in Medford, Massachusetts, in 2018.
- A computer network hack at the University of California, Santa Cruz, and DePaul University in Chicago caused campus printers to produce anti-Semitic propaganda flyers in 2016.
- Demonstrators at Hunter University in New York were reported shouting "Death to Jews" in 2015.

also argue that their schools should not do business with Israel, or make investments connected to that country. BDS backers believe that these actions will weaken Israel, causing the nation's lawmakers to agree to the formation of a separate Palestinian state.

The BDS movement has many supporters on American college campuses. Many of these individuals are quite outspoken in their hatred of Israel. It is not unusual for them to extend their hostility to Jewish students who, they assume, support the Jewish state's policies. Although criticizing Israel's or any government's policies is not anti-Semitism, extending this criticism to all Jews is. Whether or not they support Israel's policies, many college students are routinely insulted, intimidated, discriminated against, and marginalized simply because they are Jews. This mistreatment is not only demeaning but also marks Jews as *others*, socially isolates them, and limits their ability to participate in certain activities or opportunities that colleges offer. For example, on some campuses, Jewish candidates for student government are singled out and maligned. Some report that in order to participate in student government, they were required to pledge that they would not affiliate with Jewish student organizations or travel to Israel. Non-Jews are not required to do this.

In addition, progressive groups, many of which support the BDS movement, often insult or ostracize Jewish students. One such student, Arielle Mokhtarzadeh, attended a conference at the University of California, Berkeley, that supported the rights of oppressed people. She was stunned by the outpouring of anti-Semitic rhetoric expressed at the event. "I was made to feel uncomfortable and unwanted in a space that was meant to be inclusive and safe," she remembers. "It was in that moment, during that conference, that I realized that every identity and every intersection of identity was to be welcomed and championed in progressive spaces—except mine."[26] Indeed, many Jewish college students feel that they have to hide their Jewish identity in order to be accepted.

Moreover, although most college students and educators are quick to protest hostile behavior toward other minorities,

> "I was made to feel uncomfortable and unwanted in a space that was meant to be inclusive and safe. It was in that moment . . . that I realized that every identity and every intersection of identity was to be welcomed and championed in progressive spaces— except mine."[26]
>
> —Arielle Mokhtarzadeh, a Jewish college student

they are less responsive when it comes to anti-Semitic behavior. As Duke University student Tyler Fredricks explains,

> When someone wrote "No n*****s, whites only" on a Black Lives Matter flyer, the Duke community held a march where over a hundred students marched and rallied in support. They did the same thing when someone wrote a homophobic slur in the dorms. When someone wrote anti-Semitic comments on a Duke Friends of Israel flyer, there was no march, rally, or campus outrage.[27]

The Distribution of Bigoted Propaganda by Extremists on College Campuses Is on the Rise

From fall semester 2017 through spring semester 2019, extremists have increased their efforts to distribute propaganda. The numbers on the graph represent the number of incidents, by semester, of the distribution of propaganda on college campuses by white nationalist groups. This includes stickers, posters, and flyers attacking Jews and other minority groups.

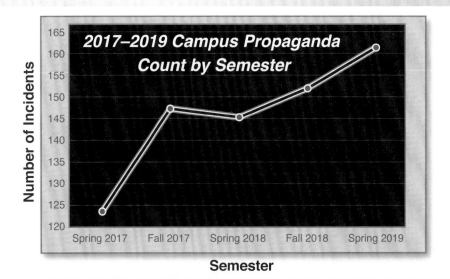

2017–2019 Campus Propaganda Count by Semester

Source: "White Supremacists Increase College Campus Recruiting Efforts for Third Straight Year," Anti-Defamation League, June 27, 2019. https://la.adl.org.

Extremists on Campus

Jewish college students also find themselves targeted by alt-right extremist groups and their followers who distribute materials targeting Jews and other minorities. For instance, in 2017, an email that threatened Jews and blacks was sent to hundreds of University of Michigan students. According to the ADL, during the 2016–2017 school year, 165 examples of white supremacy propaganda denigrating Jews in the form of posters, flyers, banners, and stickers were reported on college campuses; 292 examples were reported for the 2017–2018 school year, which is a 77 percent increase.

Moreover, these numbers appear to be growing. Between January and May 2019 alone, an additional 161 examples were identified on 122 campuses in thirty-three states. In addition to maligning Jews, this anti-Semitic propaganda serves as a recruiting tool for extremist groups. According to Keegan Hankes, an analyst with the Southern Poverty Law Center, an organization that advocates for civil rights and monitors extremist groups, "White nationalists really enjoy campus activism. They're often trying to put an intellectual veneer on things, so it makes sense to peddle that on a college campus where you're dealing with people who may be just starting to form their ideas about the world."[28]

Schools and college campuses are not always safe havens for Jews. Many Jewish young people face bias in school—and authorities do not always respond appropriately to these situations. Hostile activities targeting Jews can isolate students, negatively affect their education, and make them feel as if they are excluded and even inferior to others. That is why Hale, speaking for all Jewish students, insists, "We need change."[29]

CHAPTER THREE

Spreading Hate

Extremists spread their anti-Semitic ideology in a variety of ways. They post hateful propaganda in public places and on social media. The latter includes insulting videos and graphics, intimidating threats, and groundless conspiracy theories and accusations directed at Jews. They also use the internet to alert trolls to target Jewish individuals and groups who disagree with their views. According to Paul Singer of the New England Center for Investigative Reporting at Boston public radio station WGBH, "People who have an ideology of hate are feeling empowered. It used to be they would talk to their friends about it. Then they were sharing their ideas online and through social media. Now, they actually appear to be empowered to go step out and do stuff; they're putting up posters, they're talking to other people, and they're declaring . . . their hatred."[30]

Harassment in Public Places

In 2017 commuters on an Oregon highway were confronted by a huge banner hanging from a highway overpass that read "Jews did 9/11." Other highway banners, with phrases such as "UnJew America," "The Holocaust Is a Lie," and "Blood and Soil" (a Nazi slogan), have been displayed in Washington, California, and Colorado. One especially disturbing banner mockingly advertised a summer camp for Jewish children in which the words *concentration camp* were substituted for *summer camp*.

Since 2017, far-right extremist groups and individuals affiliated with them have been illegally displaying hateful anti-Semitic banners from highly visible locations like highway overpasses and building roof-tops. These banners, some as large as 10 feet (3 m) tall by 200 feet (61 m) long, are designed to garner widespread attention. According to the ADL, during a ten-month period from May 2017 to March 2018, ex-tremist groups used banners an average of seven times a month. Because they almost always include the group's name, logo, and website, the banners act as recruiting tools, promoting the group and its ideology. They also enhance the group's online presence because photos and videos of the banners are commonly posted on social media and are repeat-edly reposted by supporters.

Extremists spread their vitriol in other public places as well. They post anti-Semitic flyers, posters, and stickers in shopping areas, residential neighborhoods, subway stations, city streets, parks, and houses of worship, among other public areas. For in-stance, flyers that accuse Jews of being child molesters have been stuffed into Little Free Library neighborhood book exchange boxes throughout the United States, as have anti-Semitic books. Stickers displaying anti-Semitic symbols defaced a Holocaust memorial in New York State. Other such stickers and posters have been affixed to storefronts and traffic signs in multiple states, and the walls of subway stations, train cars, and buses in New York City. Extremists have even used US Postal Service mailing labels to spread propa-ganda. In October 2019 someone scrawled a series of anti-Semitic messages on these labels, which they posted all over a Brooklyn, New York, neighborhood. The messages accused Jews of poison-ing white children and commanded non-Jews to rise up and de-fend themselves. Swastikas and the number *88*, which extremists use as code for "Heil Hitler," adorned the labels.

To ensure that this material hurts, insults, and embarrasses those it is aimed at, it is often placed where Jews congregate. For example, flyers asserting that "Jews are stealing free speech" were placed on the doors of synagogues in San Francisco. Posters depicting Jews as serial rapists and others praising Hitler were affixed to the door of a synagogue in Sacramento, California. Still other flyers declaring that the Holocaust is "fake news" were posted outside synagogues in Massachusetts. Similar flyers were found outside other synagogues in Washington and Texas at the same time, indicating that the distribution of this material is often well coordinated. In the case of the posters, the ADL suspects that a national online white supremacist group coordinated the effort. According to Robert Trestan, the ADL's regional director for New England, "What we are seeing is another campaign by the white supremacist group. They put out word to their local chapters to carry out the actions to inject hatred and racism into communities."[31]

Intended to be a local resource where neighbors can exchange books with each other at no cost, Little Free Libraries have also been exploited by extremists who stuff them with anti-Semitic flyers and books.

Seeing this type of material evokes a long history of persecution in Jews, which saddens and angers them. It also serves to marginalize Jews, making them feel unwelcome in communities where they have lived for decades, as well as in the United States in general.

Spreading Hate in Cyberspace

In addition to using public areas to spread their ideology, extremists are turning to cyberspace. The popularity of the internet, and especially social media, allows prejudiced individuals to reach millions of people all over the world quickly, easily, and often anonymously. Even though many sites prohibit anti-Semitic language, it is difficult for them to monitor every posting. Anti-Semites use their organization's website, message boards, and social media sites such as Twitter, YouTube, Reddit, 4Chan, and Facebook to post anti-Jewish imagery, videos, vile jokes, vicious slurs, and allegations with no basis in fact. Followers share, repost, and retweet these items, which further expands their audience. As Lipstadt explains,

> Proponents of these noxious ideas can . . . use social media to . . . spew their hatred. With unprecedented ease, they find like-minded people and use Internet platforms to robustly amplify and spread their views. In fact, our perception that the number of antisemites and antisemitic events have markedly escalated may at least in part be governed by the ubiquity of social media. Incidents that we might not previously have heard about are now celebrated on racist websites.[32]

The ADL's Center for Extremism reports that approximately 4.2 million anti-Semitic English language tweets were tweeted and retweeted in 2018. These posts were viewed more than 10 billion times. Since trillions of tweets are posted on Twitter annually, some people discount the significance of a mere 4.2 million tweets. Most Jews, however, do not. As the ADL explains,

Of course, 4.2 million tweets is a very small number out of the trillions of tweets sent on the platform each year. But that does not negate the lived experience of Jews who have found Twitter to be a toxic environment. This number is still large enough to underscore the powerful harassment that exists and the ease with which a relative handful of users can infect our shared social media environment with negative stereotypes and conspiracy theories about Jews.[33]

Plus, because their allegations are so frequently reposted and retweeted, it is not unusual for right-wing internet and broadcast news sites to report them as actual facts. This makes anti-Semitic views seem more mainstream and acceptable to others. Social

Bias and Hate Invade Online Gaming

Online video gamers interact with each other while participating in multiplayer games. In fact, online games serve as a social platform for many participants. As with all social media, these interactions can be pleasant or involve the spreading of hatred for marginalized groups, including Jews. In 2019 the ADL sponsored a survey designed to analyze the experiences of online multiplayer gamers. It found that 19 percent of Jewish gamers who responded to the survey reported some type of harassment due to their religion while playing games online. This included being called offensive names, online stalking, threats of sexual assault and other physical violence, and discrimination by a stranger on the basis of their identity.

In addition to harassment, the study looked at whether gamers are exposed to extremist views and disinformation in online game environments. According to the survey, "Nearly a quarter of players (23) are exposed to discussions about white supremacist ideology and almost one in ten (9%) are exposed to discussions about Holocaust denial in online multiplayer games."

Anti-Defamation League, "Free to Play? Hate, Harassment, and Positive Social Experiences in Online Games." www.adl.org.

media also gives group members a way to network and communicate with one another, and an efficient way to organize and coordinate flash protests, rallies, demonstrations, and nefarious acts. Likewise, it serves as an excellent recruitment tool. Lipstadt says,

> Social media allows the extremists not only to communicate more easily with one another but also make their voices and views heard beyond their adherents. Through the various social media platforms, these hate-mongers can reach a wider audience of people, including those who might previously have not been exposed to these messages of hate. In so doing, they are normalizing expressions of hatred. Many people are uncomfortable with the white nationalists and supremacists' open adulation of Nazis, love of violence, and overt antisemitism and racism. They will not join up with them. But influenced by the extremists' spread of hatred on social media, people who might not join a supremacist organization will nonetheless begin to repeat some of their arguments.[34]

The advent of social media has enabled prejudiced individuals both to connect with each other and to spread their propaganda to a much larger degree than was ever possible before this technology. Some right-wing internet and broadcast news sites then report it as fact, making anti-Semitic views appear more mainstream.

Targeting Individual Jews

Extremists also use the internet to target and spread their hatred toward specific Jewish individuals who disagree with their views. This usually occurs in response to something the person wrote, said publicly, or posted online. However, the harassment rarely focuses on the person's views. Instead, the offender is attacked for being a Jew. To ensure maximum harassment, extremist groups use their own websites and their presence on social media to alert their followers to troll a particular Jew. For instance, when Andrew Anglin, the founder and editor of the Daily Stormer, a neo-Nazi website, read a profile of Melania Trump that Anglin thought maligned the First Lady's family, he used the group's website to reach as many of his followers as possible. He urged them to assail the writer, who, he pointed out, was a Jew. He provided them with the writer's Twitter handle, a picture of the writer, and an anti-Semitic image on which to superimpose the writer's face. He commanded, "Make sure to identify her as a Jew working against White interests, or send her a picture with the Jude star from the top of the article."[35] As a result, she was bombarded on social media with violent threats, disgusting language, and horrifying images of a figure with the targeted writer's face kneeling before a Nazi firing squad.

In many cases, the command to attack is less flagrant. Alt-right groups have created seemingly innocent symbols that they post on social media to alert those who share their ideology to go on the attack. According to the ADL, one symbol is the placing of triple parentheses around the surname of prominent Jews, that is, (((surname))). It alerts anti-Semites to the person's Jewish identity, causing them to unleash a barrage of vile slurs against this person.

Anti-Semitic groups call this symbol an echo. They use a special app to search for these echoes in order to track down targets. Jonathan Weisman, an author and the deputy editor of the

Anti-Semitism on YouTube

Felix Arvid Ulf Kjellberg, more commonly known as PewDiePie, is a young Swedish YouTube celebrity with 76 million subscribers and 20 billion views. Named by *Time* magazine in 2018 as one of the top one hundred influential people in the world, he creates and stars in satirical videos, many of which express anti-Semitic views. PewDiePie insists these videos are not anti-Semitic but rather are satires that are not meant to insult anyone.

Although these claims may be true, some people want these videos to be censored because they have the potential to influence millions of preteens and teenagers worldwide. According to Rabbi Shraga Simmons, who is also a journalist and filmmaker,

> A few of PewDiePie's online antics: giving the heil Hitler one-armed salute; creating a videotape of people dancing with signs saying "Death to All Jews"; and . . . endorsing the YouTube channel E;R that broadcasts "great videos" like lengthy Hitler speeches inter-spliced with anti-Semitic images. Based on PewDiePie's recommendation, millions of new viewers have logged onto the E;R channel, indoctrinating a generation of young citizens with anti-Semitic . . . language.

> YouTube prohibits hate speech but permits satirical content. Since PewDiePie and the producers of the E;R channel say their videos are satirical, YouTube refuses to censor them even if they spread anti-Semitic views.

Shraga Simmons, "PewDiePie and the Anti-Semitic Internet," Aish, December 16, 2018. www.aish.com.

New York Times, was targeted in this manner after he retweeted a snippet of a newspaper article that offended right-wing extremists. He explains:

> Unbeknown to, well, just about everyone, alt-right anti-Semites had created a Google plug-in that could be used to search . . . triple parentheses, since ordinary search engines do not pick up punctuation marks. Haters would slap these "echoes" around Jewish-sounding names of

people online they wanted to target. Once a target was
. . . [identified] the alt-right anti-Semitic mob could download the innocuous-sounding Coincidence Director plugin from the Google Chrome store, track down the targets like heat-seeking missiles, then swarm.[36]

Online Attacks

Many of those who are attacked are prominent Jews who have a large social media following. In most cases, they are bloggers, journalists, writers, or political commentators who challenge farright ideology. Generally, they support cultural diversity, immigrant rights, equal rights for women and minorities, gun control, and freedoms of the press, religion, and speech. Most did not support the candidacy or presidency of Donald Trump. But even conservative Jews who occasionally express an opinion with which extremists disagree have been targets of anti-Semitic harassment.

Those targeted are likely to be attacked for reporting information or airing progressive views in print, broadcast, or social media. The ADL reports that between August 2015 and July 2016, at least eight hundred journalists received some nineteen thousand anti-Semitic tweets. However, because it is difficult to track all anti-Semitic tweets, the organization says that the actual number is probably much greater. But no matter the actual number, these attacks are, at best, annoying and hurtful; at worst, they are threatening and dangerous. According to journalist Emma Green,

> "Beyond hateful language, users often photoshop journalists' faces into images from the Holocaust, like Jews lined up to get food in concentration camps or lying in bunks in barracks."[37]
>
> —Emma Green, journalist

It's hard for a number to show just how awful these tweets can be, though. Beyond hateful language, users often photoshop journalists' faces into images from the Holocaust, like Jews lined up to get food in concentration camps or lying in bunks in barracks. Users might share cartoons that depict ugly stereotypes about Jews, showing them with big noses and surrounded by piles of money.[37]

What makes matters worse is that the targeted persons are generally attacked by hundreds or even thousands of people. The attacks come in many forms, and they frequently last for weeks. Extremists frequently repost the attacks on social media so that they are seen not just by the target but by countless others, many of whom then join in the assault. As Weisman recalls,

I was served an image of the gates of Auschwitz [a Nazi concentration camp]. . . . Holocaust taunts, taunts like a path of dollar bills leading into an oven, were followed by Holocaust denial. . . . An image of a giant, bulbous-nosed, shifty puppeteer holding the strings of equally offensive caricatures of feminists, Black Lives Matter activists, Occupy Wall Street types and the like—was joined by other tropes [figures]: . . . the Jew as moneybags financier orchestrating war for Israel, the Jew as a leftist anarchist, the Jew as rapacious [greedy], the Jew as Wall Street profiteer, the Jew as weak and sniveling, the Jew as all powerful. It popped up on my computer while I edited stories or chatted with reporters. It pinged on my iPhone in the Metro and while I was driving. For weeks, more than a thousand—maybe more than two thousand—such messages flooded my electronic life, usually as Twitter notifications, but also as emails and voice mails. I hadn't known that virulent anti-Semitism still existed in America; now, I couldn't avoid it.[38]

Another Jewish journalist, Bethany Mandel, was harassed and threatened for posting an anti-Trump tweet. She, too, was bombarded with anti-Semitic slurs. One image showed her face pasted into a Nazi gas chamber with a leering Nazi officer about to release the poison gas. Another had her face looming over hundreds of concentration camp corpses. And one other image showed Hitler with the message, "Adolph's Oven Service: good for 6 million operations Guaranteed."[39] The images were sent to her and posted all over social media as well as on the websites of alt-right organizations. She was also threatened with sexual assault. Making matters worse, the harassment was continuous. One troll tweeted at her for nineteen hours straight. As the bombardment intensified, she received increasingly troubling threats. After her children were threatened and she received multiple death threats in her private Facebook mailbox, she became worried that the virtual threats might turn into physical violence. As a result, she bought a gun to protect herself and her family.

The Spreading Threat

Indeed, slurs and threats against a person's family are part and parcel of these activities. Ben Shapiro, a conservative Jewish political commentator, was sent more than seventy-four hundred anti-Semitic tweets because of comments he made criticizing

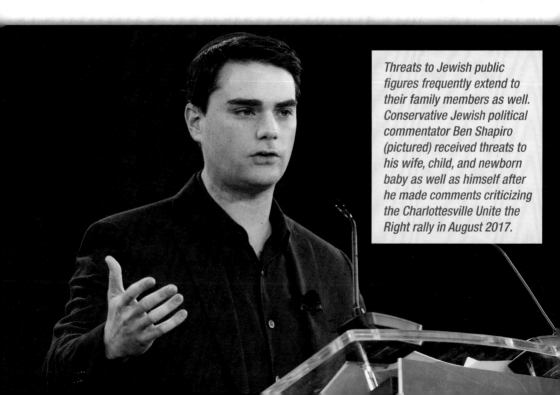

Threats to Jewish public figures frequently extend to their family members as well. Conservative Jewish political commentator Ben Shapiro (pictured) received threats to his wife, child, and newborn baby as well as himself after he made comments criticizing the Charlottesville Unite the Right rally in August 2017.

the deadly events at the Charlottesville rally. The tweets included threats to Shapiro, his wife, child, and newborn baby. He was told that all four members of his family deserved to be killed in Nazi gas chambers.

It is evident that anti-Semites have become skilled in spreading their propaganda and hatred in public places and especially in cyberspace. "What is profound is that social media is creating a public conversation that we have not seen in many, many, many years," says ADL chief Jonathan Greenblatt. "Something on 8chan or some weird thread posts on Reddit leaps onto InfoWars . . . and on to Fox News. You are seeing it spread and infiltrate, and we as Jews know what happens when weird ideas get weaponized."[40]

CHAPTER FOUR

Hate Crimes

Some Americans have gone from insulting and harassing Jews to committing hate crimes against them. Hate crimes are felonies committed against a person or property and motivated by prejudice based on race, religion, ethnicity, sexual orientation, gender, or gender identity. Hate crimes include, but are not limited to, the desecration of public and private property, physical assault, bomb and arson threats and attacks, and mass shootings. The FBI reports that 58 percent of religious-based hate crime incidents target Jews and Jewish institutions, making Jews the most frequently attacked group for these acts. Since 2016, these crimes have increased. According to the ADL, thirty-nine physical assaults against Jews were reported in 2018, including eleven fatalities. This is an increase of 105 percent between 2017 and 2018. The ADL also reports that there were 774 acts of vandalism in 2018, down from 952 incidents in 2017, but up 52 percent from 510 incidents in 2016.

As troubling as these statistics are, they may be low because many less severe incidents go unreported. Plus, numbers only tell part of the story. In reality, many of these acts produce a ripple effect. They affect not only Jewish targets but also law enforcement personnel, community members, and other people who oppose hatred. People of many faiths have condemned these acts and are showing their support for Jews in a variety of ways. For example, Gregory Locke, a New York City subway rider, witnessed firsthand how commuters of diverse backgrounds took action against anti-Semitism. Posting on his Facebook page in 2017, he described his experience in this way:

> [I] got on the subway in Manhattan tonight and found a Swastika on every advertisement and every window. The train was silent as everyone stared at each other, uncomfortable and unsure what to do. One guy got up and said, "Hand sanitizer gets rid of Sharpie. We need alcohol." He found some tissues and got to work. I've never seen so many people simultaneously reach into their bags and pockets looking for tissues and Purell. Within about two minutes, all the Nazi symbolism was gone.[41]

By fighting back against anti-Semitism in this way, people of other religions show that they support American values like freedom of religion and equal rights for all. This helps Jews to maintain their dignity and feel accepted as Americans.

Bigoted Destruction

The person who vandalized the subway car that Locke rode in committed a hate crime. Vandalizing public or private property with Nazi symbols or racial slurs is a hate crime. Drawing swastikas on public and private property, in particular, is a favorite pastime of anti-Semites who scrawl and etch swastikas on park benches, billboards, and store windows. They deface traffic signs, fences, and sidewalks with the symbol. They spray paint it in locker rooms and on the sides of buses, homes, and synagogues, among other sites.

Swastikas bring up terrible memories for Jews. The symbol evokes the systematic and senseless murder of 6 million Jews during the Holocaust, and it raises fears that this type of genocide could happen again. This is one reason anti-Semites favor the Nazi sign. Indeed, seeing a swastika displayed in a public place is especially disconcerting to Holocaust survivors and their descendants.

As Moshe Taube, a retired Jewish religious leader and Holocaust survivor explains, "This kind of evil makes me think of the Holocaust and how people can be so cruel, that there is so much evil in the world, still."[42]

No region of the United States is immune to such activity. In 2019, swastikas appeared on a road surface in a small town in New York as well as on sign posts, storefronts, fences, fire hydrants, and sidewalks in Oregon. Vandals defaced a drainage tunnel, church, private home, and elementary school in Virginia and sidewalks and buildings in many parts of California. They marred public schools in Connecticut, Illinois, Nevada, and New Jersey and college campuses throughout the nation. In October 2019 alone, eight swastikas were drawn on the walls of three buildings at Smith College in Massachusetts; on stairwells and bathroom stalls at the University of Nevada, Reno; in an elevator, a library, and on bathroom stalls at the University

> "This kind of evil makes me think of the Holocaust and how people can be so cruel, that there is so much evil in the world, still."[42]
>
> —Moshe Taube, a Holocaust survivor

In less than two weeks in 2017, hundreds of headstones were toppled or damaged in Jewish cemeteries, including this one in Philadelphia. Such attacks are one of the many ways that anti-Semites offend and intimidate Jews.

of Illinois at Urbana-Champaign; and on a staircase at Yale Law School. Even a nature trail in Brooklyn was defaced. A hiker discovered the symbol carved into a picnic table along the trail, photographed it, and posted it on Twitter with the following message: "Distressing. This is now apparently par for the course on a daily walk in NYC."[43]

Disturbing the Dead

Jewish cemeteries, graves, and tombstones have also been desecrated with swastikas, Nazi slogans, and anti-Jewish slurs. Grave sites have been disturbed and headstones damaged. In one weekend in 2017, more than five hundred headstones were toppled or damaged in just one Philadelphia cemetery. This occurred one week after 170 headstones were knocked over in St. Louis. Hundreds of headstones have also been knocked over or damaged in Jewish cemeteries in Connecticut, Illinois, Indiana, and New York.

How Young Americans View Bias Against Jews

Although large numbers of young Americans know about bias against Muslims in the United States, many are unaware of similar bias against US Jews. A recent poll conducted by the Public Religion Research Institute, in conjunction with MTV, looked at how Americans ages fifteen to twenty-four view religious bias toward Jews and Muslims. A large majority (84 percent) of survey participants recognized that Muslims face discrimination in the United States today. but only 32 percent were aware of significant discrimination against US Jews. Moreover, despite a large increase in anti-Semitic incidents, many survey respondents were unaware that bias against Jews in the United States is rising. Only 17 percent said they believed discrimination against Jews had increased in the twelve months prior to the survey, whereas 75 percent of those polled said they believed discrimination against Muslims had increased during that same twelve-month period.

In Jewish culture, cemeteries are considered to be sacred places. Jews believe that the souls of the dead remain where they are buried. Therefore, disturbing a grave site disturbs the defenseless souls of the dead. Moreover, Judaic tradition requires that the living maintain the grave sites of their loved ones. Therefore, when anti-Semites defile a Jewish cemetery, they not only offend and victimize Jews but also attack Jewish values. According to Aaron Breitbart, a researcher at the Simon Wiesenthal Center in Los Angeles, "Attacking a cemetery, especially one that is all-Jewish . . . is basically an attack on the culture, the identity of the people that cemetery represents."[44]

> "Attacking a cemetery, especially one that is all-Jewish . . . is basically an attack on the culture, the identity of the people that cemetery represents."[44]
>
> —Aaron Breitbart, a researcher at the Simon Wiesenthal Center in Los Angeles

The Danger of Being Visibly Jewish

Other hate crimes against Jews threaten the living. They involve physical assaults on visibly Jewish people. Jewish tradition requires males to keep their heads covered at all times and females to dress modestly. Many modern Jews do not follow this tradition, which makes it difficult to identify them as Jews. Orthodox (highly observant) Jews, on the other hand, follow this custom. Males wear skullcaps and other garments connected to practicing Judaism, and females dress conservatively, often covering their hair with a scarf in public. Males affiliated with some sects of Orthodox Judaism also wear other traditional apparel, including wide-brimmed hats, and many have long beards and side curls. Because these individuals are easily identifiable as Jews, anti-Semites often target them.

Orthodox Jews have been punched, slapped, choked, kicked, beaten, and attacked with bricks; they have lost teeth and had bones broken as a result of these attacks. Communities of Orthodox Jews are located throughout the United States. The largest such community is found in Brooklyn, where these types of attacks are becoming more common. According to Evan Bernstein, who directs all ADL initiatives in New York, "There's an overall climate right now that a lot of Orthodox Jews are feeling that they're being targeted either with assault or in other ways, and it's something we have to get in front of."[45]

In New York City in 2018, for example, a visibly Jewish fourteen-year-old boy was punched in the face repeatedly by a man screaming anti-Semitic slurs. At the time of the attack, the boy was walking outside a religious school, minding his own business. His only offense was being Jewish. "It's a little scary that he screamed 'Jew Boy' and then punched him," said one of the victim's classmates. "It's definitely frightening to know that there's antisemitism so close to home."[46]

Other recent assaults have been more damaging. Another 2018 attack in New York City left a fifty-two-year-old man with a broken rib, a black eye, and multiple bruises, all because he wished a stranger good morning. He recalls, "I greeted him. . . . Next thing I know he said, 'I don't like Jews, who were you talking to? I don't talk to Jews.' He put me in a headlock and I'm trying to maneuver out of him. In the meantime, I'm screaming 'Help, help.' He said, 'You don't need help. I'm going to kill you right here.'"[47]

A week earlier another visibly Jewish man suffered a broken nose and several broken ribs after being attacked in the same neighborhood. "Unfortunately there are people out there who want to kill us for one reason: Because we are a Jew,"[48] the victim's wife lamented.

Indeed, the intensity of these incidents appears to be escalating. In 2019 a visibly Jewish man was beaten on the neck, shoulders, and back with a tree limb. Others have been lashed with belts and pelted with rocks and glass bottles. In one occurrence, a rabbi was pelted with rocks and beaten with a large paving stone while he was jogging in a Brooklyn park. The attack broke the rabbi's nose, knocked out multiple teeth, and caused head injuries. "When he saw me, he jumped towards me . . . [throwing] rocks with full force towards my head," the victim, Rabbi Abraham Gopin, told reporters. "Then, he jumped on me and started

Male members of some Orthodox Jewish sects wear distinctive apparel and have long beards and side curls. These make them highly visible targets of anti-Semites who wish to bully and harass them.

to fight with me, trying to knock me in the face—probably, I would say, 20, 25, 30 times. . . . He said Jew, Jew. . . . He was for certain looking to kill. No doubt about it."[49]

Local lawmakers have denounced anti-Semitic violence and police have increased patrols in some Orthodox neighborhoods. However, these kinds of attacks can be difficult to predict or prevent. Therefore, these current incidents have become a sad reality for many visibly Jewish individuals. Sarah, an Orthodox Jew and the daughter of Holocaust survivors, explains: "It's scary because we live a good life here, and we want to live in peace and tranquility so we can be able to serve God to the best of our abilities. We don't want to be disturbed by fears, and it brings back memories of what our parents had to go through."[50]

Threats of Mass Violence

Physical assaults against Jews usually involve violence against single individuals. Some bigoted individuals, however, want to cause mass violence. They threaten arson, bombings, and mass shootings against Jewish institutions and people. They make these threats on

A Thwarted Attack

In November 2019 the FBI arrested Richard Holzer, a self-proclaimed white supremacist who allegedly planned to bomb a Colorado synagogue. FBI investigators became suspicious of Holzer after he posted a number of anti-Semitic threats on social media. An undercover agent, posing as someone who shared Holzer's views, contacted him on Facebook. Holzer responded with boasts about how he previously tried to poison the water in the synagogue and how he intended to do worse in the future.

An article in the *Washington Post* reported that Holzer admitted to hiring someone to put arsenic in the building's pipes. He said that he wanted to "make them [Jews] know they're not wanted here" and that he hated Jews "with a passion."

As part of the undercover operation, the agent offered to supply the explosives Holzer needed. He presented Holzer with two inert pipe bombs and several inert sticks of dynamite, which Holzer said he planned to detonate that night. However, he was arrested before he could do so. Holzer is one of at least a dozen people who have been arrested by the FBI for planning mass violence against Jews since the 2018 mass shooting at the Tree of Life synagogue in Pittsburgh, Pennsylvania.

Derek Hawkins, "FBI Arrests Self-Proclaimed White Supremacist in Alleged Plot to Blow Up Historic Synagogue," *Washington Post*, November 2, 2019. www.washingtonpost.com.

social media and by email and telephone. Among other incidents, in 2019 an anti-Semite tossed a Molotov cocktail at a Chicago synagogue's windows while congregants were inside praying. The attack, which failed to cause damages or injuries, was captured on video. "We saw that someone had tried to throw some sort of Molotov cocktail at the synagogue," said Rabbi David Wolkenfeld after viewing the footage. "You could see someone walking behind the building carrying some things and you could see some fire and you can see [the suspect] trying to throw the fire—some sort of bottle being thrown at the building. . . . To see somebody act in such a violent hateful way . . . was very hard to watch."[51]

In other arson attacks, fires were set at multiple Jewish institutions in New York and Massachusetts. One of these attacks endangered a rabbi and his family, who lived on-site. Although no one was injured in these acts, they caused real fear and emotional distress. As Robert Trestan, the ADL's New England regional director, tweeted, "Attacking any place of worship is a despicable act, but since these buildings are also family homes where children live, eat, and play, it is personal, scary and dangerous."[52]

As a matter of fact, many threats of mass violence are directed toward children. For instance, in a single day in 2017, in what seems to have been a well-coordinated action, Jewish schools and community centers in eleven states—Alabama, Delaware, Florida, Indiana, Maryland, Michigan, New Jersey, New York, North Carolina, Pennsylvania, and Virginia—received bomb threats. Among other threats, callers threatened to slaughter or blow the heads off of Jewish children. Betzy Lynch, the executive director of a Jewish community center in Birmingham, Alabama, answered three of these threatening calls. She explains, "It is a very disguised sort of digitized voice that indicates that there's a bomb in the building, and then there's some pretty horrific rhetoric about hurting Jewish people."[53]

According to the FBI, in 2017 more than two thousand bomb threats were made to Jewish community centers worldwide. As a result of these threats, toddlers in daycare and children and elderly Jews participating in recreational activities have repeatedly been rushed out of buildings as a precaution. Each threat and ensuing evacuation disrupts programs and services and causes anxiety in Jewish communities. "Everybody's no more than one or two degrees of separation from someone whose kid ended up on a sidewalk in front of a JCC [Jewish community center]," says Jeremy Burton, who is the head of the Jewish Community Relations Council in Boston. "It's a bit of a shock," he adds. "And maybe we are a bit naive, but we sort of maybe assumed that it was something we had mostly left behind."[54]

Mass Shootings

While most of the threats against Jewish institutions turn out to be idle, some are carried out but are thwarted by law enforcement. Still, they pose real and serious danger. In many cases, caches of ammunition and assault weapons, bulletproof armor, bomb-making materials, and explosives have been found in the homes of suspects. Moreover, not every individual who is intent on committing mass violence is caught before they destroy people's lives. In 2018 a mass shooting at the Tree of Life synagogue in Pittsburgh left eleven people dead and six injured. It was the deadliest attack against a Jewish community in US history. Six months later, another mass shooting—this time in a synagogue in Poway, California—left one person dead and

This memorial honors the victims of the 2018 mass shooting at the Tree of Life synagogue in Pittsburgh that killed eleven people and injured six. It was the deadliest attack against a Jewish community in US history.

three injured. In both incidents, the shooters proudly proclaimed their hatred for Jews on social media. The California shooter tried unsuccessfully to livestream the attack. Likewise, the Pittsburgh shooter readily told police that he wanted all Jews to die.

> "No one should have to fear going to their place of worship, and no one should be targeted for practicing the tenets of their faith."[55]
>
> —Gavin Newsom, the governor of California

Lawmakers, government officials, and religious leaders of many faiths condemned both of these attacks and expressed condolences. After the Poway attack, California's governor, Gavin Newsom, said, "We can't ignore the circumstances around this horrific incident. No one should have to fear going to their place of worship, and no one should be targeted for practicing the tenets of their faith."[55]

Since the attack on the Tree of Life synagogue, the FBI has worked to thwart further violence by arresting more than a dozen self-proclaimed white supremacists for threatening hate crimes against Jews and Jewish institutions. But others go undeterred. Consequently, violence and threats of violence have become a reality for Jews in America today. As Lipstadt declares, "I'm not a Chicken Little who's always yelling, 'It's worse than it's ever been!' But now I think it's worse than it's ever been."[56]

CHAPTER FIVE

Neither Cowed nor Complacent

For many decades—and in some cases centuries, Jews have lived and worked in the United States. They have raised families and participated in all aspects of American life. They are as American as any of their fellow citizens. But the recent resurgence of anti-Semitism has many people deeply concerned about the future.

Despite those concerns, most Jews refuse to be intimidated by hatred and violence. No matter the insults, harassment, and threats they face, they continue to live normally while adhering to Jewish values. That is not to say that they are complacent. Jewish individuals, communities, organizations, and institutions are taking steps to counter the rising tide of anti-Semitism while also doing whatever is necessary to protect themselves. Francine Roston, a Montana rabbi, explains:

> There's been this debate forever and the debate has always been, how much do we really need to care about anti-Semitism? A generation or two before me, everyone looked back at beating Hitler. They wanted to fight the Holocaust. I wanted to look forward. But now we have an obligation to work against this. I think it's about Jewish survival. We don't want Jews to feel like we need to hide. That's not just religious. It's American, right?[57]

Making Connections

One way some Jews are trying to counter anti-Semitism in their daily lives is by applying the Jewish moral value of treating others fairly and kindly. Through acts of kindness, they are reaching out to and building relationships with people of other faiths. This is what happened to Stephen Carter, an African American. When he was a boy, his family moved into a predominately white neighborhood where they were made to feel unwelcome. No one made an effort to meet the family or even speak to them, except a Jewish neighbor named Sara Kestenbaum. At the time, Carter and his family had not interacted with Jews very much. As he recalls,

> "We don't want Jews to feel like we need to hide. That's not just religious. It's American, right?"[57]
>
> —Francine Roston, a rabbi and the cofounder of the Glacier Jewish Community/B'nai Shalom in Montana's Flathead Valley

My two brothers and two sisters and I sat on the front steps, missing our playmates, as the movers carried in our furniture. Cars passed what was now our house, slowing for a look, as did people on foot. We waited for somebody to say hello, to welcome us. Nobody did. . . . I knew we were not welcome here. I knew we would not be liked here. I knew we would have no friends here. I knew we should not have moved here. . . . And all at once, a white woman arriving home from work at the house across the street from ours turned and smiled with obvious delight and waved and called out, "Welcome!" in a booming, confident voice I would come to love. She bustled into her house, only to emerge, minutes later, with a huge tray of cream cheese and jelly sandwiches, which she carried to our porch and offered around with her ready smile, simultaneously feeding and greeting the children of a family she had never met—and a black family at that—with nothing to gain for herself except perhaps the knowledge that she had done the right thing.[58]

Kestenbaum's act of kindness permanently shaped Carter's view of Jews for the better and led to both families becoming friends.

The former South Korean ambassador to the United Nations, Oh Joon, had a similar experience, which positively affected his opinion of Jews. Oh's daughter worked as an intern at Outerstuff, a sports apparel manufacturer founded and run by Sol Werdiger, an Orthodox Jew. Oh was impressed with the decency Werdiger showed all his employees. Wanting to acknowledge this, Oh invited Werdiger to lunch. During the lunch the ambassador confessed, "I have always heard negative stereotypes about Jews and I took it at face value. Then, my daughter took an internship working in your company. Throughout the year, she has been telling me how wonderful it is to work at your company."[59]

Most Jews refuse to be intimidated by hatred and violence. They continue to live normally while adhering to Jewish values and traditions, including the celebration of holidays such as Hanukkah (pictured).

Finding Common Ground

Other individuals are forging connections with non-Jews in a broader way. They are participating in seminars, conferences, and community events in which people of different faiths share their perspectives and values. It is hoped that through their participation, attendees will gain new respect for each other, find common ground, and become allies in the fight against prejudice. As author and *New York Times* op-ed editor Bari Weiss explains, "The Jewish community—2 percent of this population—cannot go at this problem alone. We have to insist that the societies of which we are part take a stand against anti-Semites because they are at the core of what erodes the fabric of civilization."[60]

New Jersey rabbi Ari Lamm, for example, recently attended an interfaith conference in Utah where he connected with Muslim, Mormon, Catholic, and Evangelical Christian leaders. He writes,

> Jews are being welcomed as never before as active participants in the national and global moral discourse. In counterpoint to the challenge of anti-Semitism, which is rearing its ugly head once again, the genuine interest in Judaism's distinctive ethical voice represents a new opportunity. . . . In a practical sense, American Jews will benefit from new friendships among communities of faith. . . . American Jews, especially from traditionally observant communities, have long suffered prejudice against the demands of their religious obligations. Whether for wearing peculiar modest garb, or for attempting to garner unobtrusive public accommodations for religious practice, Jews have faced outright cultural and legal discrimination. Other religiously conservative groups, from Muslims to Catholics to the Mormon community, regularly encounter similar outrageous challenges. American faith groups should see themselves as natural allies in a broad coalition defending our country's historic commitment to religious freedom.[61]

Speaking Out

Although some Jews are trying to counteract anti-Semitism by connecting with people of other faiths, others are working to end it by speaking out against anti-Semitic rhetoric and actions.

Young Jews, in particular, frequently face insults, harassment, and marginalization in schools and on college campuses. Whether out of embarrassment, shame, a need to fit in, or a belief that such attacks are normal, many Jews censor themselves and remain silent in the face of such bias. Others try to hide their religion or isolate themselves. Says Jewish college student Arielle Mokhtarzadeh, "We have become numb to the hateful rhetoric, we've built up a tolerance for the defamations of our character, we've given into our mother's pleas to take off our Jewish stars, we've stomached the assumptions, and we've endured in silence."[62]

Many young Jews are tired of suffering in silence. They refuse to hide their religion or allow themselves to be harassed and marginalized. Moreover, by seemingly ignoring hateful words and actions, they unwittingly help make bigotry more acceptable. To help these young people stand up for themselves and fight anti-Semitism, the ADL developed a program that teaches young people constructive and effective strategies for responding to and combating anti-Semitism with accurate information. The program, which is known as Words to Action, is an interactive educational program for Jewish middle school, high school, and college students. Through direct instruction, videos, and role playing, participants are given the skills and knowledge to recognize anti-Semitism and the best ways to counter it. As a result, they feel empowered to take action and do so more frequently. As Jewish writer Slovie Jungreis-Wolff explains,

With anti-Semitic attacks increasing in Europe and the U.S. and becoming the norm, even chic, I'm afraid that our children will not know what to say or worse—cower in shame when confronted with this spewing of animosity. Every generation has its challenges. When faced with a wall of hate, it becomes our duty to give our children the backbone and knowledge to stand proud and tall.[63]

Fighting Injustice

Some Jews are not only speaking out against anti-Semitism but are actively supporting causes that defend the rights of all marginalized people. In doing so, they are applying a Jewish moral commandment that requires Jews to strive to make the world a better place. However, by taking action against injustice, Jews make themselves targets for hatred from those who oppose these causes. In fact, shortly before the 2018 attack on the Tree of Life synagogue in Pittsburgh, the shooter posted a message

Members of the Jewish activist group Never Again Action protest US immigration policies in December 2019. The organization's goal is to prevent anything like the Holocaust from ever happening again, whether to Jews or any other population of people.

on social media stating that the reason for the attack was the congregation's support for an organization that helps immigrants. Dara Frimmer, a rabbi in Los Angeles, explains: "We can be targeted because we are Jewish and because we represent the part of America that extremists hate."[64]

Even though it would be safer to remain in the shadows and not draw the ire of hostile groups and individuals, Jewish activists refuse to back down. For instance, despite attempts to intimidate group members, between June and October 2019 a Jewish group known as Never Again Action organized more than forty protests defending the rights of immigrants and asylum seekers. In one demonstration, thirty-six young Jews were arrested for blocking the entrance of a New Jersey Immigration and Customs

Combating Anti-Semitism with Education

Despite the testaments of Holocaust survivors and documentation by historians, some anti-Semites insist that the Holocaust never happened. Many of these individuals revere Hitler and Nazism. They argue that although murdering the Jews would have been justified, these murders never occurred. They claim the Holocaust was made up by Jews in order to gain public sympathy.

These individuals spread this misinformation as a way to slander Jews. Because some young Americans know little about the Holocaust, they accept this propaganda as fact. Indeed, a 2018 survey conducted by Schoen Consulting found that the less Americans know about the Holocaust, the more likely they are to accept extremist propaganda.

In order to counter such beliefs and keep the lessons of history from being forgotten, the ADL has established Echoes and Reflections, a Holocaust awareness and education program that provides schools and teachers with Holocaust-related educational materials and resources. The program not only instructs learners about the Holocaust but also helps them to understand how an event from the past relates to the present and the future. Since the program was enacted in 2005, it has reached more than 6 million American students.

Enforcement detention center where immigrant children were being held. The group's goal is to prevent anything like the Holocaust from happening to Jews or any other group of people in the future. According to the Never Again Action website, "We know from our own history what happens when a government targets, dehumanizes and strips an entire group of people of all their civil and human rights. We understand it to be our community's obligation to stand up when we see history repeat itself and to declare, Never Again means Never Again for anybody. . . . We refuse to wait and see."[65]

While fighting injustice, Jewish activists frequently forge bonds with members of other advocacy groups that they partner with as well as with those they defend. As a result, these people often develop positive views of Jews. As Weiss writes, "We fight by waging an affirmative battle for who we are. By entering the fray for our values, for our ideas, for our ancestors, for our families, for our communities, for the generations that will come after us."[66]

Protecting Themselves

Despite efforts to end anti-Semitism, most Jews are realists. They are aware that anti-Semitism has persisted for thousands of years and will not go away easily. Although they are hopeful that their efforts will reduce bias against Jews in the future, at the present time they remain targets for hatred. Rather than live in fear, Jewish institutions, communities, and individuals are taking steps to protect themselves. "It's important that we are strong and steadfast in our spirit. We cannot allow our life to change. On the other side, we need to practically secure ourselves,"[67] explains Rabbi Zvi Konikov of Florida.

Consequently, synagogues and Jewish schools and community centers are adding or increasing security measures. Most have enacted emergency preparedness plans and conduct practice drills. As Doron Ezickson, the head of the ADL's regional office in Washington, DC, explains, "Because of the history of violence and harassment and threats against the Jewish community, all

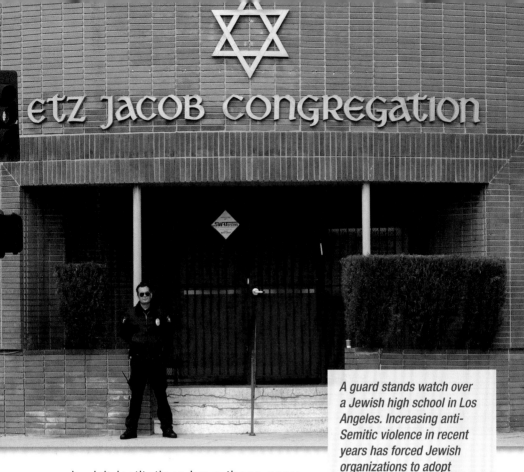

A guard stands watch over a Jewish high school in Los Angeles. Increasing anti-Semitic violence in recent years has forced Jewish organizations to adopt security measures previously thought to be unnecessary.

Jewish institutions have these security plans. All synagogues, all community centers, all preschools, all Jewish Day schools are forced, as part of their normal operative procedure, to train staff and to have procedures."[68]

Other safety measures go further, challenging Jewish houses of worship to find a balance between security and openness. The goal is to keep members safe without turning synagogues into uninviting fortresses. According to Jennifer Levin-Tavares, the executive director of Congregation Kol Tikvah in Parkland, Florida,

> If you look at the purpose of a synagogue, it's to have a sense of community. That necessarily means warmth and people feeling at home. And in order for people to feel at home, they have to feel safe and secure. . . . We constantly have to look at physical structure and see what

modifications need to happen to address any concerns that we have. . . . [However,] if your worship space feels like a prison, that's not going to be a positive experience.[69]

With security in mind, synagogues that rarely locked their doors throughout the day are now doing so. This goes against the Jewish virtue of hospitality, which teaches that synagogues are open places designed to welcome strangers, not to keep them out. However, with the uptick in anti-Semitic threats and actions, applying this principle can be dangerous. As San Francisco

Keeping European Worshippers Safe

The United States is not the only nation in which anti-Semitism is on the rise. Jews in Europe also face growing anti-Semitic threats. In fact, threats against Jewish institutions in many European countries have become so prevalent that most synagogues have taken extreme measures to fortify themselves and keep members safe. In some nations, synagogues are under constant surveillance by the police or military. In France, for instance, soldiers patrol the front of synagogues as part of that nations' national security alert system. Entering these synagogues almost feels like entering an armed camp. In addition to police and military guards, most European synagogues utilize the services of trained armed volunteer guards. It is not unusual to see a dozen or more armed individuals, wearing bulletproof vests and carrying shields, guarding European synagogues. In addition, many European synagogues have installed dedicated security command rooms. These are staffed by trained professionals who use high-tech equipment to monitor the premises and exchange information about possible threats with other synagogues in real time.

Many European synagogues have also installed specially designed doors that are strong enough to withstand gunfire or a bomb. Most have erected tall barbed wire or bulletproof fences around the building's perimeter. Despite concerns about keeping American synagogues welcoming places, many Jewish leaders predict that American synagogues may soon institute similar extreme measures.

rabbi Beth Singer explains, "We are right next to a beautiful church that keeps its doors open all day. But we have to keep ourselves locked up. We worry about the unfounded hatred of Jews and we also worry about the prevalence of heavy-duty arms that are so easily attained today."[70]

In addition, many Jewish facilities have erected perimeter fencing, replaced ordinary glass windows with bulletproof or blast-resistant glass, installed security cameras, and added panic buttons that summon police in case of an attack. Metal detectors are also becoming more common, and in some institutions, members are issued badges that must be scanned before they can enter the building. Most Jewish institutions also employ security guards or trained volunteers to monitor the entrances. Likewise, nearly all synagogues have police protection during major Jewish holidays. Moreover, orthodox communities have organized neighborhood watches and community patrols to protect residents. "None of us want this," says Rabbi Frimmer. "But we're just living in a different era."[71]

> "We are a people descended from slaves who brought the world ideas that changed the course of history. One God. Human dignity. . . . That is our legacy."[72]
>
> —Bari Weiss, an author and the *New York Times* op-ed editor

Many Challenges

Indeed, due to the current upsurge in anti-Semitism, Jews in America face many challenges. Most refuse to succumb to fear. Instead, they take steps to eliminate prejudice and protect themselves while practicing Jewish values. As Weiss writes, "There are many forces in our world insisting, again, that all Jews must die. But there is a force far, far greater than that. And that is the force of who we are. We are a people descended from slaves who brought the world ideas that changed the course of history. One God. Human dignity. . . . That is our legacy. . . . Can we make it real again? I believe that . . . we must."[72]

SOURCE NOTES

Introduction: A Growing Problem

1. Quoted in Alexandra Miller, "Jews in Charlottesville Faced a Summer of Anti-Semitism," Newsy, September 1, 2017. www.newsy.com.
2. Quoted in Paul Rosenberg, "Eight Mistakes the Media Makes About Anti-Semitism in America Today," Salon, March 21, 2019. www.salon.com.
3. Quoted in Lola Adesioye, "The Rise of Anti-Semitism in Donald Trump's America," *New Statesman*, February 23, 2017. www.newstatesman.com.
4. Deborah E. Lipstadt, *Antisemitism Here and Now*. New York: Schocken, 2019, p. xi.

Chapter One: Promises Made, Promises Broken

5. Quoted in Howard M. Sachar, *A History of the Jews in America*. New York: Vintage, 1992, p. 26.
6. Quoted in Myrna Katz Frommer and Harvey Frommer, *Growing Up Jewish in America*. New York: Harcourt Brace, 1995, p. 21.
7. Quoted in Jewish Historical Society of Greater Washington, "Restrictions," Jewish Washington: Scrapbook of an American Community. www.jhsgw.org.
8. Quoted in Frommer and Frommer, *Growing Up Jewish in America,* p. 33.
9. Quoted in Frommer and Frommer, *Growing Up Jewish in America,* p. 50.
10. Richard L. Rubin, *Jewish in America*. Purchase, NY: Park International, 2016, p. 69.
11. Quoted in Frommer and Frommer, *Growing Up Jewish in America*, p. 51.

12. Quoted in Frommer and Frommer, *Growing Up Jewish in America*, p. 80.
13. Quoted in Jessica Weiss, "Why Do White Supremacists Hate (White) Jews So Much?," Univision, August 16, 2017. www.univision.com.
14. Jonathan Weisman, *(((Semitism))): Being Jewish in America in the Age of Trump.* New York: St. Martin's, 2018, p. 46.
15. Quoted in Weiss, "Why Do White Supremacists Hate (White) Jews So Much?"
16. Quoted in Lipstadt, *Antisemitism Here and Now,* p. 51.
17. Quoted in RMuse, "American Nazis Rising as Trump's Armed Brownshirts to Target Jews," Politicus USA, December 27, 2016. www.politicususa.com.
18. Quoted in Katie Little, "Donald Trump: I am the Least Anti-Semitic Person That 'You've Ever Seen in Your Entire Life,'" CNBC, February 16, 2017. www.cnbc.com.
19. Weisman, *(((Semitism))),* p. 31.

Chapter Two: Insults, Bullying, and Discrimination on Campus

20. Quoted in Sam Berndt, "As a Jewish Teen in the Bible Belt, I Face Antisemitism All the Time," *CT Jewish Ledger*, August 2019. www.jewishledger.com.
21. Quoted in Berndt, "As a Jewish Teen in the Bible Belt, I Face Antisemitism All the Time."
22. Quoted in Susan Donaldson James, "Jewish Bullying Victim Recalls Slurs and Beatings in N.Y. School," NBC News, July 15, 2015. www.nbcnews.com.
23. Quoted in Rachel Frommer, "Education Reform Expert Warns ADL Report on Spike in Antisemitism at K–12 Schools Might Be 'Misleading,'" *The Algemeiner*, April 25, 2017. www.algemeiner.com.
24. Quoted in "ADL Welcomes Decision by Oswego County School District to Remove Holocaust Simulation Activity," Anti-Defamation League, April 3, 2017. https://nynj.adl.org.
25. Rachel Hale, "Give Students Off from School for the High Holidays," BBYO, November 6, 2018. https://azabbg.bbyo.org.

26. Quoted in Anthony Berteaux, "In the Safe Spaces on Campus, No Jews Allowed," *The Tower,* February 2016. www.thetower.org.

27. Quoted in Berteaux, "In the Safe Spaces on Campus, No Jews Allowed."

28. Quoted in Amy Crawford, "White Nationalists Are Targeting College Campuses, and These Students Are Fighting Back," Southern Poverty Law Center, May 2, 2017. www.splcenter.org.

29. Hale, "Give Students Off from School for the High Holidays."

Chapter Three: Spreading Hate

30. Arun Rath and Paul Singer, "Incidents of Anti-Semitic Propaganda on the Rise in Mass.," WGBH, September 29, 2019. www.wgbh.org.

31. Quoted in Penny Schwartz, "Anti-Semitic Flyers in Massachusetts Declare Holocaust 'Fake News,'" Cleveland Jewish News, July 16, 2019. www.clevelandjewishnews.com.

32. Lipstadt, *Antisemitism Here and Now,* p. 36.

33. Anti-Defamation League, "Quantifying Hate: A Year of Anti-Semitism on Twitter," 2019. www.adl.org.

34. Lipstadt, *Antisemitism Here and Now,* p. 36.

35. Quoted in Weisman, *(((Semitism))),* p. 129.

36. Weisman, *(((Semitism))),* p. 8.

37. Emma Green, "The Tide of Hate Directed Against Jewish Journalists," *The Atlantic*, October 19, 2016. www.theatlantic.com.

38. Weisman, *(((Semitism))),* p. 9.

39. Quoted in Weisman, *(((Semitism))),* p. 130.

40. Quoted in Weisman, *(((Semitism))),* p. 170.

Chapter Four: Hate Crimes

41. Quoted in Madison Malone Kircher, "New Yorkers Use Hand Sanitizer to Remove Subway Swastika Vandalism," *New York Magazine*, February 5, 2017. http://nymag.com.

42. Quoted in Laurie Goodstein, "'There Is Still So Much Evil': Growing Anti-Semitism Stuns American Jews," *New York Times*, October 29, 2018. www.nytimes.com.

43. Quoted in David Colon, "More Swastikas Surface in Hell's Kitchen, Newtown Creek Nature Walk," Gothamist, December 8, 2016. https://gothamist.com.

44. Quoted in Kayla Epstein, "The Disturbing History of Vandalizing Jewish Cemeteries," *Washington Post*, February 21, 2017. www.washingtonpost.com.

45. Quoted in CBS News, "Hate Crime Investigation Underway After Jewish Boy Attacked in Queens," May 9, 2018. https://newyork.cbslocal.com.

46. Quoted in CBS News, "Hate Crime Investigation Underway After Jewish Boy Attacked in Queens."

47. Quoted in CBS News, "'People Are Very, Very Nervous': Community Leaders in Brooklyn Warn of Increased Bias Attacks Against Jews," April 23, 2018. https://newyork.cbslocal.com.

48. Quoted in CBS News, "'People Are Very, Very Nervous.'"

49. Quoted in Benjamin Hart, "Brutal Assault Is Latest in String of Attacks on Religious Jews in NYC," *New York Magazine*, August 28, 2019. http://nymag.com.

50. Quoted in Ben Sales, "In Orthodox Jewish Brooklyn, a Spate of Assaults Feels All Too Familiar," Jewish Telegraphic Agency, September 3, 2019. www.jta.org.

51. Quoted in Hollie Silverman, Sheena Jones, and Susannah Cullinane, "Chicago Police on Alert After Attempted Arson and Vandalism at Synagogues," CNN, May 20, 2019. www.cnn.com.

52. Quoted in Joey Garrison, "'Somebody Out There Wants to Hurt Us': 3 Arsons at 2 Jewish Centers in 1 Week Rattles Boston Suburbs," *USA Today*, May 18, 2019. www.usatoday.com.

53. Quoted in Tovia Smith, "DHS to Help Jewish Community Centers Enhance Security Protocols," NPR, March 2, 2017. www.npr.org.

54. Quoted in Smith, "DHS to Help Jewish Community Centers Enhance Security Protocols."

55. Quoted in Spencer Kimball, "'It Was a Hate Crime': One Dead, Three Injured in Synagogue Shooting in San Diego Area," CNBC, April 27, 2019. www.cnbc.com.

56. Quoted in Goodstein, "'There Is Still So Much Evil.'"

57. Quoted in Weisman, *(((Semitism)))*, p. 187.

58. Quoted in Levi Welton, "The Best Way to Fight Negative Jewish Stereotypes," Aish, August 20, 2018. www.aish.com.

59. Quoted in Welton, "The Best Way to Fight Negative Jewish Stereotypes."

60. Bari Weiss, *How to Fight Anti-Semitism*. New York: Crown, 2019, p. 190.

61. Ari Lamm, "Judaism's Role in America Is Shifting," *Jewish Standard*, July 18, 2019. https://jewishstandard.timesofisrael.com.

62. Quoted in Berteaux, "In the Safe Spaces on Campus, No Jews Allowed."

63. Slovie Jungreis-Wolff, "The Silence of the Jews," Aish, May 25, 2019. www.aish.com.

64. Quoted in Jaweed Kaleem, "'We're Living in a Different Era': Synagogues Renew Debate over Armed Guards and Security After Pittsburgh Shooting," *Los Angeles Times*, October 28, 2018. www.latimes.com.

65. Never Again Action, "Jews Are Sounding the Alarm. Never Again Is Now." www.neveragainaction.com.

66. Weiss, *How to Fight Anti-Semitism*, p. 168.

67. Quoted in J.D. Gallop, "Space Coast Synagogues Step Up Security Measures in Wake of San Diego Shooting," *Florida Today*, April 30, 2019. www.floridatoday.com.

68. Quoted in Vanessa Romo, "After Synagogue Shooting, Religious Leaders Evaluate Security," NPR, October 31, 2018. www.npr.org.

69. Quoted in Becky Kent, "Synagogue Safety and Architecture—Synagogues Seek Balance Between Safety and Openness," Levin/Brown Architects, November 2, 2018. www.levinbrown.com.

70. Quoted in Kaleem, "'We're Living in a Different Era.'"

71. Quoted in Kaleem, "'We're Living in a Different Era.'"

72. Weiss, *How to Fight Anti-Semitism*, p. 206.

ORGANIZATIONS AND WEBSITES

Aish—www.aish.com

With over 1 million users, Aish is the world's leading Jewish content website. It provides lots of articles and news reports on Jewish life and culture, Judaism, Israel, anti-Semitism, discrimination on college campuses, and Jewish history, among other themes. It also offers podcasts and videos.

American Civil Liberties Union (ACLU)—www.aclu.org

The ACLU works to defend the constitutional rights of all Americans. Its website provides articles and reports about religious discrimination and anti-Semitism.

Anti-Defamation League (ADL)—www.adl.org

The ADL fights hatred, injustice, and all forms of bigotry, including anti-Semitism. Its website offers a wealth of information about discrimination and how to combat it.

Jewish Journal—https://jewishjournal.com

The *Jewish Journal* is a weekly Jewish newspaper that reports on all aspects of Jewish life. Readers can find podcasts, opinion pieces, reports, and articles about Jewish culture, religion, Israel, influential Jews, and anti-Semitism on its website.

Jewish Virtual Library—www.jewishvirtuallibrary.org

The Jewish Virtual Library is an online library that offers a wealth of articles, reports, fact sheets, news, time lines, and other publications related to Judaism, Jews, Jewish history, culture, anti-Semitism, US-Israel relations, and more.

Moment—https://momentmag.com

Moment is a magazine that reports on issues concerning American Jews, including articles about anti-Semitism, Judaism, and Jewish life. Current and past issues can be viewed on the magazine's website.

Southern Poverty Law Center—www.splcenter.org

The Southern Poverty Law Center fights bigotry and injustice. It provides articles and reports about religious discrimination and other topics on its website.

US Holocaust Memorial Museum—www.ushmm.org

The US Holocaust Memorial Museum is dedicated to raising the public's awareness of the Holocaust and its effects. Its website provides a Holocaust encyclopedia plus a wealth of information about Jewish history; the Holocaust, with essays by survivors; and anti-Semitism.

FOR FURTHER RESEARCH

Books

Adam Lewinsky, *Judaism*. Folcroft, PA: Mason Crest, 2017.

Wil Mara, *Religious Intolerance.* San Diego: ReferencePoint, 2020.

Peggy J. Parks, *Religious Discrimination.* San Diego: ReferencePoint, 2019.

Gary Weiner, *Anti-Semitism and the Boycott, Divestment, and Sanctions Movement*. Farmington Hills, MI: Greenhaven, 2019.

Internet Sources

Isabel Fattal, "A Brief History of Anti-Semitic Violence in America," *The Atlantic*, October 28, 2018. www.theatlantic.com.

Emma Green, "The Tide of Hate Directed Against Jewish Journalists," *The Atlantic*, October 19, 2016. www.theatlantic.com.

Scott Jaschik, "Supremacists on Campus," Inside Higher Ed, August 14, 2017. www.insidehighered.com.

Deborah Lipstadt, "Anti-Semitism Is Thriving in America," *The Atlantic*, May 3, 2019. www.theatlantic.com.

Hilary Miller, "Anti-Semitism Affecting U.S. High Schools," Louis S. Brandeis Center. https://brandeiscenter.com.

Darcy Reeder, "Growing Up Jewish in America," Medium, December 20, 2018. https://medium.com.

Erik K. Ward, "Skin in the Game: How Antisemitism Animates White Nationalism," Political Research Associates, June 29, 2017. www.politicalresearch.org.

INDEX

PICTURE CREDITS

ABOUT THE AUTHOR

Barbara Sheen is the author of 105 books for young people. She lives in New Mexico with her family. In her spare time, she likes to swim, garden, cook, walk, and read.